INSIGHT HERITAGE (

THE INQUISITOR'S PALACE

Vittoriosa

KENNETH GAMBIN

HERITAGE BOOKS

IN ASSOCIATION WITH

H Heritage Malta

2003

HOW TO GET TO THE INQUISTOR'S PALACE

By bus:
Bus nos 1, 2, 4, 6 from Valletta main bus terminus and stop at Vittoriosa bus terminus.

By car:
Main roads leading to the Three Cities and then follow the road signs to Vittoriosa and the Inquisitor's Palace.

The Inquisitor's Palace
Main Gate Str
Vittoriosa CSP 02
Malta
Tel: 2166 3731,
    2182 7006
info@heritagemalta.org

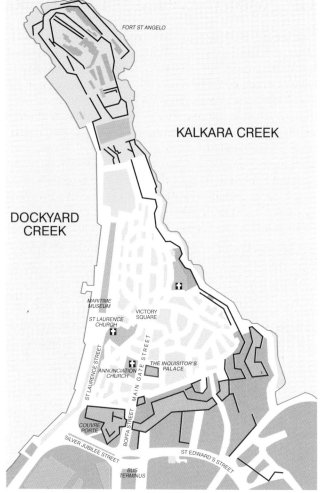

Insight Heritage Guides Series No: 4
General Editor: Louis J. Scerri

Published by Heritage Books in association with Heritage Malta

Insight Heritage Guides is a series of books intended to give an insight into aspects and sites of Malta's rich heritage, culture and traditions.

Photo Credits
Unless otherwise stated all illustrations in this book are by Daniel Cilia.
Heritage Malta, pages 6, 9, 11, 24, 25, 26, 27, 28, 29, 30
Midsea Books Collection, pages 2, 3, 6, 11, 16, 17, 21, 26, 31
Wignacourt Museum, Rabat, page 5

Printed in Malta by Gutenberg Press
Published by Heritage Books, a subsidiary of Midsea Books Ltd, Carmelites Street, Sta Venera HMR 11, in association with Heritage Malta.

Produced by Mizzi Design & Graphic Services
Photography, Daniel Cilia

ISBN: 99932-39-77-1

THE INQUISITOR'S PALACE, VITTORIOSA

The Inquisitor's Palace, sited in the heart of Vittoriosa, is one of the very few surviving examples of such palaces which could be found all over Europe and South America in the early modern period. Many simply succumbed to the ravages of time or became victims of the reactionary power unleashed by the French Revolution against the *ancien regime* and all it represented. The fact that Malta's palace, throughout its five centuries of history, always hosted high-ranking officials representing the main powers on the island, ensured its survival. The palace also survived the Second World War and the threat of modern development. Although much has been changed in the structure of the building by its successive occupants, the Inquisitor's Palace remains an architectural gem, representative of the checkered history and European heritage of the islands.

Detail of the Grand Harbour area from a map of Malta by Quintinus, 1536

The facade of the Inquisitor's Palace, constructed in 1660

THE ARRIVAL OF THE ORDER OF ST JOHN

The *Palazzo del Sant'Officio* was originally erected in the 1530s soon after the arrival of the Hospitaller Order of St John to Malta. The knights settled down and had their first administrative centre in Birgu and the building was intended to host the *Magna Curia Castellania*, that is the civil law courts.

Traces of this original building are still visible, especially the Gothic ribbed and panelled quadripartite-vaulted courtyard, similar in style to those found in other contemporary buildings in Vittoriosa.[1] Most probably the architect was Fra Diego Perez de Malfreire, *ingegnere e soprastante dell'opere*, who was the Order's engineer at the time, and who introduced this out-dated style of construction in the islands.[2] On the side of this pointed arched bay, one can also see the original entrance to the palace. The ground-floor rooms on the left side of the palace, which have a vaulted ceiling, also formed part of the *Castellania*. They are

practically the only part of the palace that remained virtually untouched through the ages. It is not known whether there was another building there previous to the Order's arrival. However, considering that Birgu was 'far from being built up' in 1530,[3] it is possible that the *Castellania* was the first building erected on the site.

The palace served as the civil law courts until 1571, when Grand Master Pietro del Monte transferred the administrative centre of the Order to Valletta as a result of the building of the new city. As a consequence the palace remained empty, as did many other buildings in Vittoriosa, whose occupants were attracted to the better opportunities of defence and employment offered in the new city. The palace thus became one of the first symbols of the shift in emphasis on the new city by the Order.

The palace did not, however, remain vacant for long. Mgr. Pietro Dusina arrived in Malta in 1574 as representative of the pope to solve a

Opposite: **The ribbed vaulted courtyard, dating back to the early 1530s**

Grand Master Pietro del Monte (1568-72)

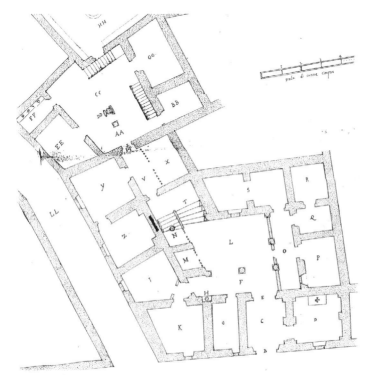

The earliest plan of the Inquisitor's Palace dating to around 1600

Top: The main internal courtyard

Above: Coat of arms of Inquisitors in the main hall of the *Piano Nobile*

Detail of a late 16th century map showing the Vittoriosa peninsula

raging dispute between Bishop Martino Royas and Grand Master La Cassiere. Dusina was also the first general inquisitor and apostolic delegate of the islands, and the grand master offered him the unused palace as the official residence of the inquisitor *pro tempore*.[4]

AN INQUISITOR'S PALACE

Previous to Dusina's arrival, the bishop of Malta had also been invested with the powers of inquisitor, and the hearing of cases used to take place in his palace. Since the *Castellania* palace had been left vacant for some years, it was not fit to host the inquisitor and his entourage. Dusina in fact sought alternative accommodation first at Fort St Elmo in Valletta and then at the Dominican convent in Vittoriosa before actually settling in the palace.[5] This took place only after the basic rehabilitation works had been carried out.[6] From then on it became known as the Inquisitor's Palace and it became the official residence of all 61 of Dusina's successors until 1798.

A LIVING BUILDING

Buildings have lives in time, and those lives are interwoven with the lives of the people who use them. They change or grow in response to the changes in the exigencies of their users and reflect them. The Inquisitor's Palace was not built at one go. Various inquisitors and other subsequent occupants modified sections of the building as they saw fit, sometimes demolishing or altering parts which had been erected by their immediate predecessors and constructing other sections to suit their requirements and tastes. This is the main reason why today the palace is a complicated building with a rather haphazard interior. There is no apparent order since there was never a general master plan for it as a whole, and whenever expansion took place it was basically unprogrammed. For instance, the left wing of the lower floor, the former *Castellania*, was slowly transformed into an area for

The oven (*above*) and the kitchen area of the palace (*left*)

services such as the kitchen, storage of wood and coal, and toilets. The inquisitors preferred to reside in the upper floors of the *Piano Nobile*. This was normal practice throughout Europe, first of all for the privacy it afforded, but also because their dampness precluded the use of the ground-floor area as apartments.

Although the palace passed through the hands of so many different 'masters' they all shared the same cultural values of clerical baroque Roman society, which put a lot of emphasis on façade effect, protocol, and the order of precedence. The palace was considered the outward sign of the splendour of a family or institution, and was used to impress and command deference, even if it masked onerous debts. By 1798, when the Inquisition was abolished from Malta by Napoleon, the palace had become radically different from the way it was in the late sixteenth century. Surviving plans from these periods are barely comparable to each other and to the present building. By means of one project after another, the inquisitors transformed the building into a typical *palazzo romano*. Not without problems, however.

The facade of the palace in the 1930s

A breached bell-shaped well used as a toilet of one of the prison cells.

Opposite: The majestic main staircase, designed by Carapecchia in 1733

FINANCIAL PROBLEMS

The need of funds for the upkeep of the palace was constant throughout its 224-year history as the official residence of the inquisitors. The Maltese Holy Office was far from a rich institution. Its financial well-being depended almost exclusively on its landed property, mainly the fields of Girgenti in the limits of Siġġiewi, which Inquisitor Pietro Dusina had confiscated from the heretic Matteo Falson in 1574.

In the first decades of the Holy Office it was normal practice to mete out fiscal penalties to those found guilty of unorthodox practices. Considering the financial situation of the Holy Office, various inquisitors relied on fiscal sentences as a source of revenue. The end-of-year balance sheet was so unsustainable that Inquisitor Ettore Diotallevi (1605-07) was asked to curtail his monthly salary to 50 *scudi* to make good for the deficit, and this reduction had to be backdated to when he was appointed inquisitor.[7]

The practice of resorting to financial sentences was rarely used after the sixteenth century since the Holy Congregation of Rome did not want to appear to be interested in financial gains or material wealth.[8] By the first decades of the seventeenth century, the practice of expropriation and of fiscal penalties had dwindled to a minimum in all the Roman Inquisition tribunals across Europe,[9] including Malta.

This policy put more pressure on the inquisitors. The situation was not so critical throughout the whole history of the Inquisition in Malta. However, the financial position of the Holy Office was one of the toughest problems which local inquisitors had to tackle. Even in the eighteenth century, as Inquisitor Giovanni Francesco Stoppani (1731-35) pointed out to Rome, the normal vote allocated to the Maltese tribunal was barely enough to be able to respect its basic obligations – such as the salaries of Inquisition officials – let alone

An artistic impression of the palace of 1696

carry out the necessary repairs to the palace.[10] The need for improvements was never-ending and the *Computa* (financial records) of the Holy Office are replete with references to sums of money *spesi in servizio del palazzo Apostolico, in riparamenti fatti nel palazzo,* or *per lo stato del Palazzo.*

Various inquisitors went to great lengths to ensure some sort of financial assistance from Rome. They usually suggested using the money collected by the local branch of the *Reverenda Fabbrica di San Pietro* to see to the urgent repairs. However, this procedure needed a special permission from the pope himself. The great effort at centralization made by Rome after the Council of Trent in its attempt to control everything concerning the Church's administration, not least its finances,

was leaving its mark. Bureaucracy reigned supreme.

Structural changes and repairs in the palace would not have been possible at all without the special grants made by various popes to local inquisitors. Two popes were particularly benevolent and understanding of the needs of the Maltese tribunal: Alexander VII (1655-67) and Innocent XII (1691-1700). Both of them, as Fabio Chigi (1634-39) and Antonio Pignatelli (1646-49) respectively, had served as inquisitors in Malta, and therefore understood perfectly well the particular difficulties of the local Holy Office.

Shortage of funds was so chronic that some inquisitors forked out money of their own to ensure that the much-needed improvements were carried out. This also explains the frequent repairs needed by the palace: lack of money was always a great obstacle towards affecting the most needed repairs in the most efficient way. Reconstructions or alterations were nearly always carried out with the budget deficit in mind. This, in the long run, proved to be more expensive since repairs had to be repeated over and over again within a relatively short span of time, rather than being done properly as a long-term project, with due allowance being given to natural wear and tear.

Inquisitors Fabio Chigi and Antonio Pignatelli, later Pope Alexander VII and Pope Innocent XII

Left: The Council of Trent

Opposite: Girgenti Palace

11

ALEXANDRO VII ET INNOCENTIO XII
SVMMIS PONTIFICIBVS
QVOD HAS AEDES OLIM PRAESENTIA DEIN SVPPEDITATIS SVMPTIBVS
EXORNAVERINT
IOANNES FRANCISCVS STVPPANVS INQVISITOR GENERALIS
SVBSTRVCTIS CLEMENTIS PAPAE XII BENEFICENTIA
AD EARVNDEM AMPLIOREM ASCENSVM
NOVIS SCALIS
PONI CVRAVIT

FROM CASACCIA TO PALAZZO

In the first decades of the Holy Office in Malta the palace was not in a good shape and it was not considered as a very hospitable place in which to live by the Inquisition's high-ranking dignitaries. Letters by local inquisitors to Rome are replete with references about the need for repairs and embellishments in the palace, which lacked space for all the staff as well as prisons for its inmates, and was still attached structurally to abutting buildings. In fact the term used to describe the building was *casa* or *casaccia* and not 'palace'. The word *palazzo* started to be used later on, especially from the mid-seventeenth century onwards, only after a series of alterations and additions had been carried out.

Most inquisitors, being of Italian noble descent, were used to much better premises from where to conduct their work. Upon his arrival in Malta, Inquisitor Innocenzo del Bufalo (1595-98) found the place totally unfit for his job and preferred to reside in Valletta instead.[11] As a result of del Bufalo's decision, the palace deteriorated further and his successor, Antonio Ortensio (1598-1600), had to carry out what appears to be one of the first refurbishments of the palace. The kitchen and the oven were practically reconstructed anew, and there is a reference to a chapel.[12]

In its early years, the palace had a totally different layout from that of today. The chapel was located instead of the present main entrance. The right wing still did not make part of the building. Instead the edifice stretched far back on its left-hand side. It also had a third courtyard, formerly a garden, but which around 1600 was being used to rear chickens.

The story of how the palace eventually gained its present size and shape has still some hazy parts. Probably demand for land increased considerably in Vittoriosa after the Order settled in the harbour area, which became the centre of all the island's economic and cultural activity. After a slump in the population of Vittoriosa, when the Order transferred its headquarters to Valletta in 1571, there was a marked increase in the first decades of the seventeenth century owing to steady immigration from the countryside.[13]

Opposite: **Another view of the architecture of the main staircase**

Holy figures on the wall of a prison cell which was probably used as a chapel

Views of the garden with the uncovered walkway connecting the two sides of the palace

The market value of property presumably shot up once again as a result of increased demand, and possibly some inquisitors found it more convenient to sell off some of the Holy Office's land and concentrate on a smaller, but safer and more decent, building.

During the first half of the seventeenth century, the palace was not even a block of building of its own; it was structurally joined with private houses on both its flanks. Some inquisitors found this a useful escape route when the palace was attacked by angry hordes of knights in their attempt to free any of their fellow members who had been arrested. Initial plans to isolate the palace from all surrounding buildings were made in 1619 by Inquisitor Fabio Della Lagonessa, who was given the green light to proceed with his attempt of buying the buildings touching with the palace.[14] But nothing materialized from these plans.

The first major overhaul of the palace took place in the 1630s under Inquisitor Fabio Chigi.[15] Lamenting that the palace was barely large enough for him and his entourage,[16] he modified it in several parts and transformed the entire structure into a more habitable place, providing initial indications of his taste for artistic patronage and building mania which peak when he was elected pope as Alexander VII.[17] Initially he wanted to live in Valletta,[18] and his decision to reside at the Vittoriosa palace was only motivated by his desire not to be involved in the continuous intrigues of the Hospitallers in the capital city. But, having decided to reside in Vittoriosa, he made sure that the palace was improved to his liking.

Employing funds accumulated by his predecessors,[19] but possibly also some of his own, Chigi began to commission work soon after his arrival. He had a garden built by demolishing some small rooms in the major courtyard, thus opening up a larger internal square, which he surrounded with a high wall to block all vision from nearby houses. He then designed the layout of the garden itself, applying the principles of Vitruvius, Columella, and Varrone, and which he planted with lemon, orange, and pomegranate trees. He even designed its fountain and passage-ways.[20]

Chigi also built a turret which connected the rooms of the upper floor with those of his household on the ground floor. He also built a 'very high tower' from which he could see the sea and where he used to rest, study, and possibly observe the skies with his Galileian telescope. He also planned to purchase an adjacent house to isolate the palace from neighbouring structures and to enlarge the 'inadequate' prisons. At one point, he was so fed up with the bureaucratic difficulties and constant delays from Rome that he simply gave up all hope of ever obtaining the necessary permits.[21]

Chigi's plans were in fact only finalized by his successor Gio. Battista Gori Pannellini, who purchased the house that touched the palace on its right flank and erected seven prison cells. Three large ones on one side looked onto the street, while four smaller ones on the other side of a central corridor faced the garden. He constructed his private quarters over the cells.[22] The three large cells and the private apartments are still extant today. It is not known when the remaining four cells,

The section of the prison constructed by Inquisitor Gori Pannellini in the 1640s (*above*), upon which he constructed his private quarters (*left*)

Top: One of the halls on the *Piano Nobile*

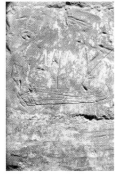

Above: One of the many graffiti of ships in the prison

of which today only the doorways remain, were demolished, but most probably this occurred when the British military occupiers of the palace (1800-1906) decided to make space for a 'racket court'.

Gori Pannellini's project meant that only the left flank of the palace remained annexed to the neighbouring buildings. In 1653 Inquisitor Federico Borromeo once again proposed the idea that the palace should be completely isolated. The plan for this project, described as *maestrevole e di molto profitto*, was based on the preliminary draft designed by Fabio Chigi – who by then had became cardinal.[23] Chigi even continued to push forward this idea during his papacy. In 1656 he gave his full support to Inquisitor Giulio degli Oddi who wanted to carry on with his predecessor's plan to isolate the building.[24] This time the

attempt was successful. The remaining property touching with the palace was eventually purchased by Inquisitor Gerolamo Casanate, and the edifice was finally isolated from all other buildings in 1658.

The isolation of the palace marked a great improvement as regards the security of the palace itself, especially *vis-à-vis* the opportunity for prisoners to escape. However, ironically, it created a problem for the inquisitors themselves when they wanted to escape from the palace from angry knights. In fact in 1659, soon after the purchase had been made, the *Suprema* suggested to Casanate that he should consider digging an underground tunnel for such instances.[25] It is not known whether this suggestion was eventually taken up but no trace of any tunnel has ever been found.

Another sore point was the façade, which became totally inadequate for the palace as it developed structurally on both its sides. Initial plans had been drawn under Federico Borromeo (1653-54), but the present symmetrical design was built in 1660 by Inquisitor Casanate with the approval of Pope Alexander VII (Chigi), who described the design as 'noble and modest at the same time'.[26] Although it has been claimed that the architect was Francesco Buonamici, the resident architect of the Order between 1635 and 1659,[27] the façade can be safely attributed to one of his assistants, Francesco Sammut. The entry of 11 December 1660 of the *Computa* of the Holy Office states: '*Havemo pagato a Maestro Francesco Sammut, architetto, scudi trenta, quali se li pagano per diversi disegni da lui fatti della facciata del Palazzo del S. Offizio, e per l'assistenza nella fabrica della medesima facciata*'.[28]

Another general upheaval occurred in January 1693, when, during the tenure of office of Inquisitor Francesco Acquaviva d'Aragona, Malta was struck by a terrible earthquake. The palace, along with many other buildings such as the Cathedral in Mdina, was heavily damaged. Acquaviva obtained permission from Pope Innocent XII (as Antonio Pignatelli himself resident in the palace from 1646 to 1649) to use 400 *scudi* to see to the most urgent repairs to ensure the safety of the building, especially as regards the roofs.[29] In reality the repairs undertaken were more extensive since 665 *scudi* were spent.[30]

Further structural repairs and alterations following the earthquake of 1693 had to be undertaken by Acquaviva's successor, Tommaso Ruffo (1694-98), who enlarged the edifice by building the upper part of the left wing of the palace – still

known as the Ruffo Apartments. These he built following the strict Roman sequence of stairs, hall, anteroom, audience room, and bedroom. The apartment was the most important part of the palace; a private territory where single celibate men of high rank not only ate and slept but also carried out the important business of diplomacy and representation. Ruffo also erected the chapel in the *Piano Nobile*, at a time when a chapel within a 'house' was considered a sign of ostentation and, therefore, a status symbol. Pope Innocent XII approved the structural alterations *con particolare compiacimento*.[31] The construction works were considerable, since no less than 1,246 *scudi* were spent to complete of the whole project.[32] The construction of the Ruffo Apartments

The door lintel commemorating the 1733 project of Inquisitor Stoppani

The chapel, built by Inquisitor Tommaso Ruffo in 1696

The timber panelled ceilings and frescoed walls of the *Piano Nobile*

Light and shade near the Bibliotheca

meant that the original Inquisitor's Quarters built by Gori Pannellini in the 1640s were left empty, and were therefore designated for some of the staff of the palace. By 1733 they were transformed into the office of the Inquisition's auditor;[33] in 1757 they were used to host the meetings of the congregation of the Holy Office.[34]

No sooner that a part of the palace had been repaired that damages cropped up in other areas. In 1698 the roof of the chancery (which had been redone only twenty years before by Inquisitor Giacomo Cantelmo)[35] was in such a critical state that the officials of the tribunal warned Inquisitor Giacinto Messerano that they would not be setting another step there unless the necessary repairs were carried out. The chancery had also to be enlarged since it could not accommodate the ever-increasing documents of the Inquisition.[36] Messerano also ordered *Maestro Gio. Battista Caloriti Pittore*, known as *il*

Nigro, one of the followers of Mattia Preti,[37] to paint the friezes of the three main halls of the *Piano Nobile*, including the coat-of-arms of the inquisitors.[38] Prior to the beginning of the actual work, Messerano calculated that the entire works would cost around 600 *scudi*. The structural changes were extensive. Besides the rebuilding of the prison cells, the chancery and the adjoining rooms of the *Piano Nobile* were entirely reconstructed, together with a new library and a torture chamber. However, owing to the fact that *il giuditio de periti ordinariamente fallace in questa materia*, the expense actually came to 1,100 *scudi*.[39] Once again all the works were approved by Pope Innocent XII.

Structural problems surfaced again in 1707. This time the roof of the tribunal itself needed urgent attention, to the extent that the hearing of cases could not proceed normally. Money represented the usual problem and Inquisitor Giacomo Caracciolo had to carry out some repairs at his own personal expense. Other repairs were once more needed and approved in 1718, since the palace had not really been taken care of during the three years in which the post of inquisitor had been left vacant (1715-18).[40] The chapel was also completely refurbished in the 1720s, during the tenure of office of Antonio Ruffo (1720-28).[41]

Even the inquisitor's private quarters suffered the passing of the years. In 1729 Inquisitor Fabrizio Serbelloni pointed out that the beamed ceiling of his bedroom was completely rotten and needed immediate repairs.[42] The same complaint had been aired by Fabio Chigi a century earlier,[43] and by Inquisitor Angelo Ranuzzi in 1668.[44]

But, without any doubt, the prison cells represented the main structural problems. Various inquisitors took the initiative to repair the prisons, especially before the mid-seventeenth century, when the palace still did not have a proper prison complex, and the prison cells were spread in various locations on the ground- and first-floor levels. In 1605 Inquisitor Ettore

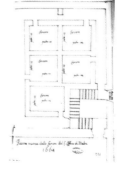

Top: One of the communal prison cells

Above: A 1664 plan for the prison complex

The chapel dedicated to St Peter the Martyr

Diotallevi set the tune which was followed by many of his successors.[45] By 1610 the prisons were once more so much in need of a general refurbishment that Inquisitor Evangelista Carbonese, as a desperate fund-raising measure, proposed to increase the number of familiars of the Inquisition against payment, so that he could use the money collected to repair the cells. His proposal was turned down.[46]

The prison complex continued to present perennial problems. Escapes continued to occur, while the humidity of some of the cells deteriorated the iron bars, the wooden doors, and even the limestone walls, which needed incessant attention. Permissions to refurbish the cells were constantly requested in vain by the inquisitors. By 1673 the prison cells had became so insecure that Inquisitor Ranuccio Pallavicino obtained permission from Rome to commute prison sentences as long as they were less harsh.[47] The music had not changed at all 25 years later. In 1698 Inquisitor Giacinto Messerano reported that the cells were in such a critical condition that one prisoner, Pietro Liccini, managed to dig his way through the wall eight times in less than a year. The prisons, in fact, were practically entirely reconstructed.[48] Although far from solving all the problems related to the prisons, Messerano's was the last known major intervention that finally provided the palace with a prison complex worthy of its name. No other major developments concerning the prisons are recorded in the eighteenth century.

The palace as a whole, however, underwent other changes. The last major overhaul appears to have been carried out by Inquisitor Giovanni Francesco Stoppani in the 1730s.

Stoppani planned to replace the beamed ceilings and refurbish the three halls of the *Piano Nobile*, since they were not *in stato da poter soffrir il peso cha hanno anzi chiaramente si vede che minacciano rovina*.[49] While the works were in progress, unexpected abundant rains caused one of the walls of the main hall to absorb much more water than usual. As a result it collapsed onto the main staircase and Stoppani had to seek temporary alternative accommodation for himself and his staff for six months in a nearby residence.

Stoppani was quick to react and he embarked on a more extensive and ambitious project: to construct a new majestic entrance to the palace and a main staircase *con simetria e decoro corrispondente al corpo dell'edifizio*, ensuring that it became the centre-

Opposite: **Scenes from prison: a communal cell (*top*), a graffiti of a ship (*middle left*), Arabic graffiti (*middle right*), sanitary facilities (*bottom left*), and prison window (*bottom right*)**

Inside one of the prison cells

The original design of Romano Carapecchia for the main staircase

A Baroque decoration in the staircase

piece of the whole edifice. Stoppani also built the *Bibliotheca*, the stairs which lead to the second floor, enlarged the family's quarters, gave a facelift to the garden, constructed a passageway which links the Ruffo Apartments to the auditor's offices, and a new drainage system. All details of this massive project were recorded by the meticulous *procuratore* of the Holy Office, Baldassare Ciantar.[50] The sum spent was a massive 5,243 *scudi*.

Undoubtedly Stoppani embarked on such an extensive project also to increase his and the office's status. In other words, the project was also undertaken for what it symbolized, for its contribution to a particular image which the inquisitor wanted to project of himself and of the Inquisition in general.[51] Conspicuous consumption was a value widely shared by eighteenth-century European society as a form of communication: 'to be distinguished from others, whether equals (and therefore rivals), or inferiors'.[52] In this case the immediate intended receivers of this message would have been the bishop of Malta and the grand master; more the latter than the former. Stoppani grasped this opportunity to transform the palace to satisfy his requirements and aspirations and to demonstrate his power.

It was precisely the staircase which acted as the definite architectural point of reference in which this social discourse took place.[53] It was in itself an important vehicle of diplomacy since one's social standing was acknowledged precisely by the point in the staircase in which one was received by the inquisitor. The paying of calls, in fact, was so important that it required specific instruction books setting forth its principles and details. The inquisitors of Malta had their own manual for such occasions.[54]

Another important aspect of this entire undertaking was the mind behind such a project: the architect who designed it, who was none other than the famous Romano Carapecchia, who was paid 102 *scudi per aver fatto il disegno della scala, ed assistito diverse volte nell'esequtione del suo disegno.*[55]

Carapecchia's plan of 1733 also allows us to make some wider observations on the palace and its history. It is certain that the level above the *Piano Nobile* had been built before 1733 (though certainly not before 1696 since it is not included in that year's plan). This dispels the idea that this floor was an extension constructed in the early nineteenth century by the British. In 1733 the room above the chancery was, in fact, used by the secretary of the inquisitor.[56] It is not yet known when the upper floor of the palace was constructed, but it is possible that it was the work of Inquisitor Giacomo

Caracciolo (1706-10) and architect Giovanni Barbara in 1707.[57] The fact that no official records referring to this work have been recorded could mean that Caracciolo had paid for it from his own pocket and then simply put a plaque in the main staircase as a record of his munificence.

Apparently the palace underwent another minor upheaval in 1745 during the inquisitorship of Paolo Passionei. That year 591 *scudi* were paid for the *fabbrica dell'accrescimento della scaletta per andare su le terrazze del Palazzo Apostolico … stanze fatte di nuovo, muro divisorio su le terrazze … e belvedere*.[58]

Even though the palace had been isolated from all other buildings in the seventeenth century, secrecy, the fulcrum of the entire institution, continued to constitute a problem for the tribunal at least up to the mid-eighteenth century. In 1757

Inquisitor Gregorio Salviati wrote to Rome about three small shops which were located right in front of the palace. They were providing an excellent excuse for *persone oziose* who wanted to check what was going on in the palace, and who was being summoned at the tribunal, to the extent that some people were refusing to come to the palace to testify because of their presence. This was causing great difficulties to the proper functioning of the Holy Office and Salviati suggested two possible solutions. The first one was that he be allowed to exchange these three shops with some houses which the tribunal had in Vittoriosa, near

Top: The staircase

Above: Manuscript extract showing Carapecchia's payment of 102 *scudi* for his work

Marble plaque commemorating Inquistor G. Caracciolo's personal expense in the palace

The window which was a threat to inquisitorial procedural secrecy

Right: **General Napoleon Bonaparte abolished the Inquisition from Malta**

The date of the last Inquisitor remained empty after the arrival of the French

Bottom: **Defaced coat-of-arms**

JULIUS DE CARPINEO
ROMANUS AB AN. 1793
AD AN.

the palace. Alternatively the Inquisition could purchase the shops as soon as the financial situation of the Holy Office allowed it to do so. The *Suprema* was not against such a plan,[59] but it is not known if he followed it up or not.

Parts of the palace continued to change function with the passing of the years and the different whims of the various inquisitors. Salviati also decided to transfer the chancery back to the ground floor, in the first room on the right of the main door of the palace. The chancery had been located on the *Piano Nobile* by Inquisitor Messerano in 1700 but it had subsequently been relocated on the ground floor. It was transferred to the *Piano Nobile* once again during inquisitorship of Paolo Passionei (1743-54). However, the new location created a lot of embarrassment for those who wanted to make reports to the Holy Office without revealing their presence in the palace to third parties, since they could meet other persons as they were walking up the stairs to the chancery. To eliminate these difficulties, Salviati re-located the chancery on the ground floor.[60]

A similar problem concerned the back of the palace. A private mezzanine had one of its windows facing the window of the room where the meetings of the council of consultors of the Holy Office used to take place. The street was so narrow that the proceedings in the room could be easily overheard from the window on the other side of the road. The consultors could also be recognized, to the detriment of the *secreti e cautela colle quali [il tribunale] suol trattare gli affari*. The Holy Office, therefore, had to hire the said mezzanine temporarily until it could

possibly be bought and sub-leased to responsible persons.[61]

No other major structural changes are recorded for the second half of the eighteenth century. Apparently inquisitors were at last happy with their facilities. Compared to the hectic activity of previous years, this inactivity or staticity could also possibly indicate the wearing out of the Inquisition as an institution and its decreasing relevance. The presence of the Holy Office in Malta came to a close in 1798. In line with the revolutionary ideals heralded by the Enlightenment and the French Revolution, General Napoleon Bonaparte abolished the Inquisition from the islands in June 1798. The last inquisitor, Giulio Carpegna, had left the previous month.

THE FRENCH INTERLUDE

During the brief French occupation, all the property of the Inquisition passed to the civil government. The palace was used as headquarters of the Cottonera district, under the leadership of Commander Noblet.[62] It is possible that the French erased a number of coat-of-arms of the Inquisition and of various popes which used to adorn the 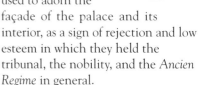  façade of the palace and its interior, as a sign of rejection and low esteem in which they held the tribunal, the nobility, and the *Ancien Regime* in general.

THE BRITISH COLONIAL PERIOD

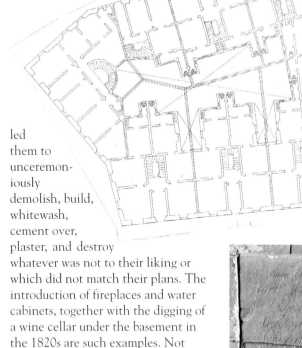

When the British colonised the island, the military authorities took over the palace. At first it was used as a military hospital,[63] but soon the premises were considered inadequate. By the 1830s the army had transformed the palace into a 'mess-house for the officers of the British garrison stationed at the barracks of Fort St Michael in Senglea',[64] to be used as a residence separate from that of their troops when they were off duty. The army occupied the palace as 'perpetual user without payment' with the condition that the building had to revert to the civil government if it was no longer wanted for military purposes.[65] In the meantime, as the nineteenth century rolled on and the living memories of those who had previously visited, worked, or knew anything factual about the palace progressively diminished, all kinds of myths about the building started to crop up in the popular imagination.

The British forces did not show much respect for the building or what it represented and the palace suffered extensive damage throughout their tenure. The military looked at it from a very practical point of view, which led them to unceremoniously demolish, build, whitewash, cement over, plaster, and destroy whatever was not to their liking or which did not match their plans. The introduction of fireplaces and water cabinets, together with the digging of a wine cellar under the basement in the 1820s are such examples. Not even the tribunal room was spared: part of one of its walls was demolished to accommodate a toilet. Every hall of the *Piano Nobile* was divided in two by a middle wall and transformed into officers' offices and quarters, while soot from the newly-constructed fireplaces covered the friezes of the coat-of-arms of the inquisitors, which had been previously covered with thick layers of whitewash. Some parts were changed to the extent that they were rendered unrecognizable. For instance, the cupola of the chapel was demolished to construct a corridor connecting rooms on the fifth level. Many of these changes are still visible, although by now they have become an essential part of the travailed history of the building.

The palace was eventually exchanged by the military for three other sites in Valletta.[66] This contract came under heavy fire from the elected members of the Council of

Top: **The 1908 plan to demolish the palace and erect private apartments instead**

Above: **A British graffito in one of the prison cells**

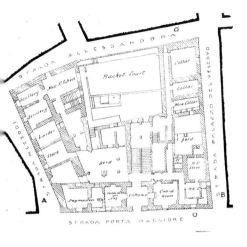

A plan of the how the palace was used by the British in the 19th century

The halls of the *Piano Nobile* during restoration in the late 1920s

Government of Malta and was made the subject of hot discussion in the sitting of 6 May 1908. They demanded and insisted that the contract of the transfer of the palace to the civil government be declared null and void.

In fact it emerged that by 1900 the military authorities had no further use for the palace. According to an order in council of 1896, any building which had been requisitioned by the military and which was no longer needed by the latter (and which had not been built by finances contributed by the British public) had to revert automatically to the civil authorities without any conditions whatsoever. But since the military

had earmarked three other buildings in Valletta which were more useful for its purposes, they 'set up a plan' with the civil authorities so that the latter would request the palace from the military with the excuse that it was needed to be converted into a government school. In this manner the clause of 1896 would not apply and the military could exchange the palace with the three other sites as planned. In reality the authorities did not know how to utilize the building. To add insult to injury, the palace was valued £1,800 more than the property that the military got in exchange, and the civil government agreed that this balance should be indebted to the Maltese public!

THE INQUISITOR'S PALACE

The elected members were simply furious at this deal, which the chief secretary to the government assured had been 'straightforward and fair'. It seemed clear and obvious to them that this entire operation was nothing more than a maneouvre by the British authorities to accommodate their needs with blatant abuse of the law and against the interests of the Maltese people – which it was their duty to safeguard – and at their expense! They defined the transfer as 'scandalous, alarming, erroneous, disastrous, and an insult', accusing the civil authorities of incompetence and the military of arrogance. The fact that the other property which the military obtained in return was not used as an officers' mess (as the palace had been used before) only reinforced their conviction and strengthened their case. However, in spite of the considerable energy with which the elected members presented this resolution and the convincing arguments that they brought forward, the resolution was rejected.[67]

Fortunately for the government, it appears that the elected members were not aware that while they were discussing the hand-over of the palace, plans were being drawn up by the Public Works Office to demolish it and construct a block of government apartments instead. It is not known what led to the abandonment of this plan. However, the fact that nothing was ever done in the palace by the civil government in the following twenty years supports the view of the elected members that the authorities never really had any plans for the building. In fact Treasury officials were trying to lease the building to third parties. In their opinion, this appeared the best solution to the 'awkward

problem as to how the palace could be utilized', and a good way of 'getting rid of a white elephant'. Moreover, this matter 'has been made the subject of various questions in parliament', and 'the building has only been a source of expense since it was taken over from the W.D. in 1903'.[68] The deal had indeed been a 'frame-up' to the detriment of the Maltese people in the best possible British colonial style.

THE MUSEUMS DEPARTMENT - I

The Antiquities Committee had been consulted on the case of the palace and in 1924 they had come forward with the following proposals, signed by Sir Temi Zammit:
(a) The Inquisitor's Palace in Vittoriosa is a very important historical building and as such worth to be repaired and preserved;
(b) The necessary work for that object should be carried out by the government as early as possible and before proceeding to any

The first Museum Annual Report on the palace, signed by Vincenzo Bonello in 1926

APPENDIX C.

Report of the Curator of the Art Section.

THE MUSEUM – ART SECTION.
25th. June, 1926.

Sir,
I have the honour to submit the report on the working of the Fine Arts Section for the financial year 1925-26.

INQUISITOR'S PALACE.

This most interesting monument which bears evidence of the Mediaeval, the Renaissance and the Baroque periods is being freed, as far as possible, of the abundant traces of the awkward and mischievous meddling of man, during the last century. In almost every room of the first and second floors, mural decorations have been discovered. They consist chiefly of rich decorative friezes bearing very often the coat of arms of inquisitors, of popes or the Inquisition's peculiar emblem. Some inscriptions have also been met with. The chapel, once very richly carved and gilded, has also been set free of the plaster that concealed its carvings, but unhappily, very little could be recovered, owing to previous diligent scraping of every jutting ornament. Generally speaking, architectural and decorative elements that could not disappear under a whitewash, were hewn off to obtain a plain even surface. Only when the whitewash was removed from the main room to discover the rich armorial frieze, it was found that the entrance to the chapel was originally adorned with a bold jutting architectural façade consisting of an entablature surmounted with scrolls and festoons laid down over two pilasters. Of this sumptuous decoration, diligently smoothed evenly with the wall's surface, only an outline remains due to the discontinued painted wall surface. The supports or cartouches that enclosed the big inscription facing the main staircase were likewise cut off and scraped. Modern partition-walls were pulled down and walled up staircases reopened. Other partition-walls have still to be demolished and other subterranean places cleared out.

The main staircase (*above*) and garden (*below*) during restoration in the 1930s

administrative disposal of the building;

(c)   Provided that the palace be not given on long lease there is no objection to the government letting the same under the condition that no structural alterations be effected without the knowledge and consent of the Antiquities Committee whose representatives shall be allowed, at any time, access to the building.[69]

In any case, although it is still not clear how the hand-over actually took place, the palace finally passed into the hands of the Museums Department in 1926, when it became part of the Fine Arts Section, whose curator was Vincenzo Bonello. Between 1926 and 1936 Bonello freed the palace from 'the abundant traces of the awkward and mischievous meddling of man during the last century'.

Bonello carried out valid basic work to restore to the palace some of its lost dignity and respect. He made sure that all the friezes of the *Piano Nobile* were uncovered from the thick layers of whitewash that the British had covered them with. The entrance to the chapel, which 'was originally adorned with a bold jutting architectural façade consisting of an entablature surmounted with scrolls and festoons laid down over two pilasters' was, as far as possible, reconstructed, since every jutting ornament had been 'diligently scraped' in order to obtain a flat surface. The cupola of the chapel was reconstructed. All partition walls and fireplaces installed in the large halls were removed and maximum care was taken to ensure that some of the original architectural features of the palace were restored. The main courtyard, which was divided by a high partition wall separating a small garden from a 'racket court' with a cement floor, was once more re-converted into a garden. Bonello even carried out some excavations in the garden and in a well which yielded some interesting pieces of pottery, and finally put to an end the legend of the palace having a knife-pit, which turned out to be simply a normal bell-shaped well. The work of Vincenzo Bonello was continued by Antonio Sciortino in 1937. He continued on his predecessor's footsteps until 1939, when all work ground to a halt because of the outbreak of the Second World War.[70]

Opposite: The cupola of the chapel rebuilt by Vincenzo Bonello

THE INQUISITION IN MALTA

The Tribunal Room, known as the *Camera Secreta*

A list of the patentees and officials of the Inquisition of 1665

Through its work, the Tribunal of the Inquisition shaped the history, society, culture and mentality of early modern Europe down to modern times. There were three separate Inquisition Tribunals: the Medieval, the Spanish, and the Roman. In Malta we are mainly concerned with the Roman Inquisition, better known as the Holy Office, which was established by Pope Paul III in 1542. It was inspired by the recent success of the Spanish Inquisition, and its main aim was to oppose the increasingly popular Protestant doctrines, which were considered as a major threat for the Catholic Church.

The Holy Office was officially set up in Malta in 1574 after Grand Master La Cassiere sought the help of the Vatican to act as an intermediary in a quarrel between himself and Bishop Martin Royas. The pope sent Mgr. Pietro Dusina as his representative, who had to

An inquisitorial sentence of 1639 by Inquisitor Gori Pannellini

act as both apostolic visitor and inquisitor.

The Inquisition acted as a watchdog against all kinds of heretical practices and beliefs. One could either be denounced or else appear spontaneously to admit guilt. It enjoyed jurisdiction over everyone in such a way that the Roman Catholic Church was able to exert great influence over all sectors of Maltese society.

In the late sixteenth century the main worries of the Inquisition were heretical behaviour and the reading of prohibited books because of the influence of Protestantism. Once this had died out, however, the Holy Office turned its attention towards reforming the popular religious culture of the masses. The most common 'heresies' included blasphemy, apostasy to Islam during slavery, bigamy (especially by sailors or their wives), solicitation during confession, and a myriad of magical beliefs which the inquisitors grouped together under the title of 'superstitions'. Popular culture contrasted a lot with the official Church doctrines, but many of those who sinned were not always aware that they were acting against the precepts of the Catholic Church.

The absolute majority of the sentences, especially for first-time offenders, were of a spiritual nature, including fasting and prayer. Recidivists, however, could face imprisonment, exemplary shameful punishments such as hearing mass kneeling near the main door of a church, or physical punishments such as public beatings, rowing on the galleys or exile. Conditions in the prisons of the Inquisition were humane and compared very well with contemporary prisons. Torture, which could not last longer than thirty minutes, was used rarely and was mild when compared to that used by secular governments. The accused would have his hands tied behind his back with a rope attached to a pulley in the ceiling. He would then be pulled up in the air and let down for a number of times.

The Maltese Tribunal served as an ideal stepping-stone for those prelates who aimed to advance in their ecclesiastical career. Those who performed well during their tenure of office as inquisitors of Malta generally managed to obtain higher posts. Twenty-seven out of the 62 (Italian) inquisitors of Malta became cardinals, and two of them were even elected popes. Fabio Chigi (1634-39) became Pope Alexander VII (1655-67), while Antonio Pignatelli (1646-49) governed the Church as Pope Innocent XII (1691-1700).

An official edict of an appointment of an Inquisitor

THE SECOND WORLD WAR AND AFTER

The Dominican church opposite the palace, destroyed during World War II

The sacristy of the chapel

The church of the Annunciation and the convent of the Dominican friars, right across the road from the palace, were destroyed by enemy bombing in 1941. For the friars to continue with their apostolic work they needed a substitute for their convent and the palace was earmarked for this purpose. It welcomed the first group of friars on 18 December 1942, after some necessary repairs and maintenance had been carried out to host its new occupants.[71]

The Dominicans transformed the two main halls of the *Piano Nobile* into a chapel and the tribunal room into the sacristy. In this chapel they celebrated not only the day-to-day liturgical rites, but also the more important ritual festivities. At one time it was feared that these services would have to be stopped because of an outbreak of bubonic plague owing to the great conglomeration of people in confined spaces and lack of adequate sanitary facilities. But daily fumigation by the health department in the chapel made sure that the spiritual services offered by the Dominicans at the palace continued uninterrupted throughout the war and after. In fact, although lying so close to the dockyard, an area greatly exposed to the innumerable enemy air raids that razed so many buildings to the ground, the palace miraculously survived the war practically unscathed, even if it went through some very close shaves. On 26 July 1943, for example, a bomb exploded right in front of the building.[72]

The Dominicans remained in the palace until 1954, by which time their convent had been reconstructed. The palace, however, continued to be used

The plaque commemorating the opening of the Folklore Museum in 1981

as a chapel until 1960, when the church of the Annunciation was finally completed.

THE MUSEUMS DEPARTMENT - II

Once the Dominicans had vacated the building, the palace returned under the direct responsibility of the Museums Department. Rehabilitation works continued in the 1960s, and the building was finally opened to the general public as the Inquisitor's Palace on 21 February 1966.[73]

In the late 1970s the upper floor of the palace was converted into a museum exhibiting objects of 'popular arts, crafts, and customs',[74] and it was officially opened to the public as a Folklore Museum on 5 December 1981.[75] Unfortunately, however, the palace slowly fell into disuse, and by the late 1980s only the *Piano Nobile* and the prison sections remained accessible to the public.

NATIONAL MUSEUM OF ETHNOGRAPHY

In 1992 the ethnography section was set up within the Museums Department under Dr Carmel Cassar, who recruited a group of student volunteers. Emphasis was made from the start on the basic restoration of the artefacts and the building and the cataloguing and inventory of the entire collection, including the costumes. The palace was chosen as the headquarters of the section and it was decided that it should be converted into an ethnographic museum focusing on the popular devotions and religious cultural values latent in Maltese ethnic identity. The palace was the ideal place to emphasize such a concept, since the *raison d'etre* of the Inquisition was precisely to model and enforce popular devotions and religious culture and make them conform to the official doctrines sanctioned by the Catholic Church and imposed by the Council of Trent (1545-63). Since 1992 a new life is slowly being injected into the Inquisitor's Palace. A careful historical reconstruction of the palace, based on extensive research on documentation present in Inquisition archives both in Malta and at the Vatican, is presently under way.

Gideon and the Angel **by Salvatore Busuttil (1798-1854)**

PERMANENT EXHIBITION

The Eucharist and the Confessional
The cult of the Eucharist (here represented by a nineteenth century wooden gilt tabernacle) was a response to Protestant attacks on transubstantiation (the conversion of bread and wine in the Eucharist into the body and blood of Christ), the Mass, and the special position of the priesthood. Similarly, the invention of the confessional was a direct response to Protestant criticisms of the institution of confession and the sacrament of penance. It conveyed the positive message that repentance was a continuous business and in fact it became a very powerful tool for social control. The exhibited confessional dates back to the seventeenth century and was brought from the chapel of Fort Ricasoli in 1995.

Right: Mid-eighteenth century wooden gilt Maltese clock. The palace used to be adorned with similar pieces of furniture. In 1709, for instance a new *orologio e sua cassa* were bought to adorn the halls (*Computa 1710-46*, f.15).

Saints and Pulpit

The Protestant Reformation brought a 'crisis of canonisations' in its wake, as no further saints were proclaimed after 1523 for a period of 65 years. With renewed confidence following the Council of Trent, the Congregation of Sacred Rites and Ceremonies was established in 1588. Among other things, it was to be the forum for the reformed and standardised canonisation procedure. The Church offered new saints and new images which emphasised the achievements of the Catholic Reformation. In a widely illiterate age, paintings and the pulpit were the most important tools in the hands of the clergy through which to put forward their message and direct the popular culture of the masses through the official channels. The pulpit is a Maltese work of the eighteenth century in rococo style. It was donated by the Santa Scholastica nunnery of Vittoriosa in 1995.

Left: Mid-eighteenth century Maltese wooden portable altar in the form of a bureau-bookcase with gilded mouldings in baroque and rococo styles. It was purchased in 1930-31 as a gorgeous and excellent example of wood carving and gilding.

Scenes from the Via Sagra

For Catholics, Easter is the most important time of the year since the Catholic Faith revolves around the passion, death and resurrection of Christ. Eastertide devotions, rituals a traditions increased in the sixteenth century as a result of the Council of Trent. The growing devotion to the passion of Christ was also an exercise in identity affirmation by southern European Catholics as against the Protestantism of the North. To play with such figurines, therefore, came also to signify a demonstration of one religiosity and allegiance; an indicati that the efforts of the Holy Office to make people conform, at least outwardly, to the official doctrines of the Church, was leaving its mark. The fourteen Stations of the Cross o exhibit were modelled in clay by Mr Emanuel Peregin from Valletta, who donated them to the museum in 199

NOTES

1 L. Mahoney, 'Ecclesiastical architecture', in L. Bugeja, M. Buhagiar, S. Fiorini (eds), *Birgu – A Maltese maritime city*, ii (Malta, 1993), 399, 404.

2 Id., *5000 years of architecture in Malta* (Malta, 1996), 61, 321.

3 S. Fiorini, 'Demographical aspects of Birgu up to 1800', in *Birgu*, i, 228.

4 N[ational] L[ibrary] M[alta], Lib. 325, f. 3v.

5 A. Bonnici, *Storja ta' l-Inkizizzjoni ta' Malta*, i (Malta, 1990), 87-8; M. Fsadni, *Id-Dumnikani fir-Rabat u fil-Birgu sa l-1620* (Malta, 1974), 238.

6 A[rchives of the] I[nquisition in] M[alta], Proc. Vol. Prae IB, ff. 37r-v.

7 AIM, Corr. 1, f. 253, 14 July 1606.

8 Ibid., 2, f. 71, 8 May 1610.

9 V. Lavenia, 'I beni dell'eretico, le entrate dell'inquisitore. Inquisizione romana e confisca, secc. XVI-XVII' in *L'Inquisizione e gli storici: Un cantiere aperto* (Rome, 1999).

10 AIM, Corr. 94, ff. 286-7v, 16 February 1732.

11 AIM, Conti, unpaginated.

12 Ibid., [1597-98], unpaginated; Ibid., [1598-1600].

13 Fiorini, 244-5.

14 AIM, Corr. 3, f. 233, 11 August 1619.

15 See K. Gambin, 'Fabio Chigi 1634-39: Inquisitor-Missionary and Tridentine reformer (M.A. disertation, University of Malta, 1997).

16 B[iblioteca] A[postolica] V[aticana], [Archivio] Chigi, A.I.3, f. 240, 15 November 1634.

17 R. Krautheimer, *The Rome of Alexander VII, 1655-1667* (Princeton, 1985).

18 BAV, Chigi, a.I.32, f. 338, 11 May 1634.

19 V. Borg, *Fabio Chigi Apostolic Delegate in Malta 1634-1639* (Vatican City, 1967), 499.

20 BAV Chigi, A.III.55, f. 453, 1 April 1635; BAV, Chigi, A.I.3, f. 326, 28 May 1635; f. 278, 24 February 1635; ff. 335r-v, 16 June 1635.

21 BAV, Chigi, A.I.3, f. 326, 28 May 1635; A.I.3, f. 277, 23 February 1635; f. 349, 17 July 1635; A.I.4, f. 371, 1 May 1638.

22 BAV, Chigi, A.III.57, f. 125, 30 November 1640.

23 AIM, Corr. 9, f. 219, 24 May 1653.

24 Ibid.,10, f. 68, 25 March 1656; f. 91, 5 August 1656; f. 124, 10 February 1657.

25 Ibid., ff. 235-v, 29 March 1659.

26 Ibid.,11, f. 22, 22 May 1660.

27 Mahoney, 'Secular architecture', in *Birgu*, ii, 401, 446.

28 AIM, Computa 1658-1709, f. 10v. See Borg, 112.

29 AIM, Corr. 15, f. 178, 28 March 1693.

30 AIM, Computa 1658-1709, f. 124.

31 AIM, Corr. 16, f. 50, 3 August 1697.

32 AIM, Computa 1658-1709, f. 135.

33 J. Azzopardi and W. Zammit, 'Inquisitor's Palace in Vittoriosa: Discovery of three original plans in Rome', *Treasures of Malta*, Easter 1999, 19.

34 AIM, Corr. 30, f. 376, 17 December 1757.

35 AIM, Computa 1658-1709, f. 70.

36 AIM, Corr. 94, f. 3v, 9 August 1698; ff. 9-v, 25 October 1698.

37 E. Corace (ed.), *Mattia Preti: From drawing to colour* (Rome, 1996), 231-3.

38 AIM, Computa 1658-1709, f. 146v.

39 AIM, Corr. 94, f. 26v-7v, 13 February 1700.

40 Ibid., 21, f. 147, 20 August 1718; Corr. 94, f. 212, 23 July 1718.

41 AIM, Computa 1710-46, ff. 170, 189-99.

42 AIM, Corr. 94, f. 236v, 1 October 1729.

43 BAV, Chigi, a.I.4, f. 31v, 7 December 1634.

44 AIM, Computa 1658-1709, f. 29.

45 Corr. 1, f. 205, 10 September 1605.

46 Ibid., 2, f. 71, 8 May 1610.

47 Ibid., 12, ff. 232r-v, 6 May 1673.

48 Ibid., 94, f. 3v, 9 August 1698; ff. 9r-v, 25 October 1698; f. 26v, 13 February 1700.

49 AIM, Memorie 5, ff. 165-6v.

50 Ibid., ff. 352-82v, Libro delli pagamenti fatti dal procuratore del Sant Officio alli lavoratori cha hanno lavorato nel Palazzo Apostolico del Sant Officio di Malta per il risarcimento dei soffitti fatti nuovi nella Cancellaria, Sala dei Staffieri, ed Anticamera, nuova loggia, nuova fabrica, ed altro bisognevole dal dì 24 Luglio 1733, sin'oggi dì 16 Luglio 1734.

51 P. Burke, 'Res et verba. Conspicuous consumption in the early modern world', in J. Brewer and R. Porter (eds.), *Consumption and the world of goods* (London-New York, 1994), 149.

52 Id., *The historical anthropology of early modern Italy* (Cambridge, 1987), 132-6.

53 P. Waddy, *Seventeenth century Roman palaces. Use and the art of the plan* (New York, 1990), 3-8.

54 NLM, Lib. 23, f. 4, Trattamenti dell'Inquisitore nel ricevere e rendere le visite. For the entire project, see K. Gambin, 'Carapecchia's intervention at the Inquisitor's Palace', *Malta Archaeological Review* (2000), 34-9.

55 AIM, Mem.5, f. 370v.

56   Ibid., f. 165.
57   AIM, Corr. 94, ff. 134-5, 19 October 1707.
58   AIM, Computa 1710-46, ff. 441-v.
59   AIM, Corr.96, ff. 103-4, 19 December 1757; Corr.30, f. 376, 21 January 1758.
60   Ibid., 30, f. 139, 20 March 1756.
61   Ibid., 96, ff. 103-4, 19 December 1757.
62   C. Testa, *The French in Malta* (Malta, 1998), 595.
63   P. Cassar, *Medical History of Malta* (London, 1964), 98.
64   G. Badger, *Description of Malta and Gozo* (Malta, 1838), 213.
65   *Debates of the Council of Government of Malta*, 1890-91, xiv, 6-7, 15 October 1890.
66   Ibid, 1917-21, xxxix, 2183-4, 7 May 1921.
67   Ibid., 1908-09, xxxiii, 1239-70, 1449, 6 May 1908.
68   Govt. Files, Treasury 1171/23.
69   Ibid.
70   *Museum Annual Reports*, 1926-38.
71   M. Fsadni, *Id-Dumnikani Maltin fi żmien il-gwerra 1939-1945* (Malta, 1977), 147-8.
72   Interview with Fr Mikiel Fsadni at the Inquisitor's Palace on 27 March 2001; Fsadni, 150, 207.
73   Govt. Files PW 9/53, MUS 10/59; Museum Annual Report 1967.
74   Reports on the working of Government Departments: Museums, 1 April 1976 – 13 August 1977.
75   *The Times of Malta*, 7 December 1981, 15; *L-Orizzont*, 7 December 1981, 24.

The Gothic ribbed and panelled quadripartite vaults of the main courtyard, probably constructed by architect Fra Diego Perez de Malfreire in the early 1530s